THE ULTIMATE TAROT COLORING BOOK

INCLUDING ALL 78 CARDS

WITH EXPLANATIONS

Modern
ZEN PRESS

Thank you so much for purchasing

THE ULTIMATE TAROT COLORING BOOK!

This book is an absolute labor of love and we hope you enjoy coloring it as much as we enjoyed making it.

If you do, please consider leaving a review on Amazon.

It would mean the world to a small business like ours.

If you have any questions, notes or remarks, don't hesistate to contact us on Instagram:

@modernzenpress

A NOTE ON PAPER:

Amazon's selection of paper is most suitable for colored pencils, crayons and alcohol-based markers. If you're planning on using wet mediums, we advise you to lay a sheet of paper behind the page you are coloring in order to prevent any bleed-through that might occur.

Copyright © 2021 by Modern Zen Press

1st REVISED EDITION

All rights reserved. No part of this book may be reproduced or used in any manner without written permission from the copyright holder.

A BRIEF OVERVIEW

THE TAROT

The TAROT is a set of 78 playing cards, devided into the MAJOR and MINOR ARCANA. According to legend it first emerged in ancient Egypt, however there is no definite proof of its true origin.

The tarot as we know it today is to be understood as the symbolic language of our subconscious, as a kind of mirror of our soul. Therefore, reading tarot cards has always been a popular way of making the hidden content of our human consciousness accessible.

THE RIDER-WAITE TAROT

The RIDER-WAITE TAROT DECK is the most popular and most used tarot deck. It was created by Arthur Edward Waite and Pamela Colman Smith in 1909. Its imagery was influenced by the 19th-century magician and occultist Eliphas Levi, as well as by the teachings of the *Hermetic Order of the Golden Dawn*.

The images' details and backgrounds feature abundant symbolism to be interpreted in different ways.

COLORING THE CARDS

This book allows you to familiarize yourself with all the 78 cards of the Rider-Waite tarot in a playful and enjoyable way. There is no wrong way to use this book. Go through the cards in order, color the images that speak to you in the moment, or just open a page at random. And if you ask the book a question before you do so, the accuracy of the "random" card might surprise you.

Happy Coloring!

MAJOR ARCANA

The Fool (0)

The Magician (1)

The High Priestess (2)

The Empress (3)

The Emperor (4)

The Hierophant (5)

The Lovers (6)

The Chariot (7)

Strength (8)

The Hermit (9)

Wheel of Fortune (10)

Justice (11)

The Hanged Man (12)

Death (13)

Temperance (14)

The Devil (15)

The Tower (16)

The Star (17)

The Moon (18)

The Sun (19)

Judgement (20)

The World (21)

MINOR ARCANA

SUIT OF WANDS:

Ace of Wands
Two of Wands
Three of Wands
Four of Wands
Five of Wands
Six of Wands
Seven of Wands
Eight of Wands
Nine of Wands
Ten of Wands
Page of Wands
Knight of Wands
Queen of Wands
King of Wands

SUIT OF CUPS:

Ace of Cups
Two of Cups
Three of Cups
Four of Cups
Five of Cups
Six of Cups
Seven of Cups
Eight of Cups
Nine of Cups
Ten of Cups
Page of Cups
Knight of Cups
Queen of Cups
King of Cups

SUIT OF SWORDS:

Ace of Swords
Two of Swords
Three of Swords
Four of Swords
Five of Swords
Six of Swords
Seven of Swords
Eight of Swords
Nine of Swords
Ten of Swords
Page of Swords
Knight of Swords
Queen of Swords
King of Swords

SUIT OF PENTACLES:

Ace of Pentacles
Two of Pentacles
Three of Pentacles
Four of Pentacles
Five of Pentacles
Six of Pentacles
Seven of Pentacles
Eight of Pentacles
Nine of Pentacles
Ten of Pentacles
Page of Pentacles
Knight of Pentacles
Queen of Pentacles
King of Pentacles

MAJOR ARCANA

The **22 cards** of the **MAJOR ARCANA** are the so-called **symbol cards**. They show us great events and important stages in life. They can alert us to upheavals and display topics that are of great concern to us. They are images of our souls that appeal to our subconscious.

More recently, the sequence of the major arcana is also known as the **hero's journey**. It symbolizes a spiritual journey that every person goes through in the course of his life.

THE FOOL

Indifference · Independence · Breaking out of Constraints

The fool stands for the curious child in us who knows no boundaries and tries everything. We have to be optimistic at times and overcome our own limits. At court, the court jester was an important courtly authority outside of social norms – he was the only one who had a fool's freedom. The fool had to be intelligent to slip into the role of a supposedly natural fool.

Only he could appropriately criticize the king without running the risk of losing his head for his criticism. The fool lives in the present and demands spiritual freedom. We sometimes need this naivety and curiosity in order to free ourselves from overwhelming problems and to gain a different and better view of our life situation.

THE FOOL.

THE MAGICIAN

Courage · Creativity · Spirit of Adventure · A New Relationship · A New Job

His magical powers are based on the control of the 4 elements that lie in front of him: the staff of fire, the water goblet, the air sword and the pentacle of the earth. He makes his will a reality. To do this, he needs inspiration, energy and control over matter. His mystery and power are based on the merging of his subconscious with the consciousness of making his will real. He subordinates himself to the magical laws and creates a balance between the elementary powers. He receives and gives at the same time. He is the channel between the non-physical and the physical world.

The magician uses all possibilities of communication, proceeds playfully and dynamically and uses his mind, his imagination, his courage and his body. He is full of confidence, masculinity, potency and sexuality. In the field of tension between ignorance and knowledge, he shows adaptability. But it can also be treacherous and often lead us to dangerous places and into hopeless situations.

THE MAGICIAN.

THE HIGH PRIESTESS

Intuition · Inner Voice · Soul · Inspiration

The high priestess stands for female intuition, faith, emotionality and willingness to compromise. Negative aspects are mysticism, naivety and too much passivity. Overall, the symbols are very contrasting. Earthly and heavenly, science and belief, evident and hidden. The contradicting aspects of life have to be constantly reevaluated and brought into harmony with one another – a burden and task of femininity. It is not about rational knowledge but about intelligent and intuitive decisions.

The card is usually interpreted in such a way that the questioner is reminded to skillfully solve problems, tasks and conflicts despite incomplete information. The high priestess reminds us that there is ALWAYS a way out and to trust in the strength of your own intuition.

THE HIGH PRIESTESS

THE EMPRESS

Growth · Love · Feelings · Fertility · Pregnancy

The empress symbolizes the maternal principle of becoming and passing away, the eternal and everlasting cycle of life. The 12 stars stand for the 12 constellations of the astrological zodiac, the 7 pearls around her neck represent the 7 old planets. Thus, the empress also represents the creative power of the entire universe. The universe constantly creates new life somewhere, but also allows old life to die. The empress is surrounded by whole grain, lush forest and a bubbling brook – all symbols of the goodness of mother nature. The empress calls on us to let our skills and knowledge grow. We should fit into the cycle of growth and decay and continuously evolve. If we allow space for this growth process, body, mind and soul will reap ripe fruits.

III

THE EMPRESS.

THE EMPEROR

Father Figure · Rationality · Vitality · Strength · Growing Up

The emperor is responsible for his domain. He protects himself with strong armor and subordinates himself to his task. He is characterized by stability and rigor. He must be incorruptible and must always successfully defend his power and area of responsibility. The ruler reminds us that we cannot always blame others for our situation. Whoever blames others gives power to others. You are only powerful if you take responsibility for your own life. Look out for new paths. Sometimes this also includes a certain amount of internal discipline, which always pays off. In his left hand the ruler holds the golden orb as a symbol of his domain. The ankh in his right hand symbolizes persistence and his spiritual authority.

IV

THE EMPEROR.

THE HIEROPHANT

Search for Meaning · Moral · Religion · Tradition

The hierophant is the spiritual head and mediator between the sacred and the profane. He conveys the meaning of life, the origin of being. As the head of the priestly caste, he is also the guardian of knowledge and values. A hierophant can be a priest, spiritual teacher or shaman.

The crosses on his drapery symbolize the union of two opposites. Sometimes we have to reflect on old values or pass them on to others. The hierophant often sacrifices personal freedom in favor of his calling. The tarot hierophant reminds us that our goals are based on essential beliefs. Thus, this tarot card is also a card of your own self-confidence.

V

THE HIEROPHANT

THE LOVERS

Heart Decisions · Love · Desire · Partnership

The card doesn't just represent the love between a man and a woman. The mountain separates the sexes and emphasizes the mutual differences, which form two poles of one unity. Behind the woman is the fertility tree with a snake as a symbol of sin and of the problems that arise in relationships on a daily basis. In the background behind the man you can see a burning bush symbolizing the male seed for procreation.

The angel watches over both, protecting and blessing – he is the guardian and keeper of the union of these opposites. Often this tarot card also signals responsibility in connection with far-reaching decisions in which one has to weigh between several options. One should fully accept a matter as the natural order while listening to one's heart.

VI

THE LOVERS.

THE CHARIOT

Triumph · Goals in Life · New Beginnings

The chariot is an invitation to pursue your goals consistently and with discipline – in the end there is integration and success. The two animals represent the polarities that have to be overcome. The driver's gaze is always directed straight ahead towards his goal. Only he takes on responsibility for the company and only he is the sole recipient of the expected glory. Sometimes he has to let go of his familiar surroundings and is not allowed to look back. The starry sky as a chariot cover symbolizes the personal universe, so it is the chariot of our life's path that must always be led towards the goal and the desired success. It is important not to lose any time and to take advantage of outside help from time to time.

The chariot also warns not to overestimate our own strength and to prove and improve our skills in holding the reins every day. Driving our life vehicle requires a willingness to learn. Even small setbacks and disabilities will not be completely avoidable on this tightrope act.

VII

THE CHARIOT.

STRENGTH

Life Force · Passion · Enjoyment · Courage

The strength tarot card represents two opposites – the petite young woman and the wild lion. Two souls live in us – a gentle feminine and an animal masculine part.

The card stands for the task of constructively connecting the animal nature with the acquired civilized mental powers. This is only possible through an adoring recognition of one's own savagery. At the same time, the absolute will is crucial to lovingly curb archaic impulses and transform them to maximum enjoyment.

Both sides together result in strength. A single aspect would be imperfect and weak. Sometimes we believe that we lack the necessary strength to carry out our tasks – this tarot card teaches us that we already have this strength within us, but due to an unfavorable balance of these aspects of our soul it can happen that we suppress one of these sides and thereby hinder ourselves.

VIII

STRENGTH.

THE HERMIT

Withdrawal · Introspection · Meditation
Cosmic Forces

The hermit follows his inner light and does not allow himself to be distracted by external influences. He goes his way and seeks wisdom within. He makes his identity clear in his thoughts, actions and feelings. This self-reflection helps the hermit focus on his goal. The hermit determines his own goals, he makes his own independent decisions – but he does not have to isolate himself from his fellow men. He practices following his inner voice and living his own identity.

In a state of seclusion, he cannot run away from himself – he confronts himself with his own fears and compulsions. The hermit represents the confrontation with one's self – from this state he draws his strength. This tarot card identifies a phase or situation in life in which the application of this philosophy is helpful.

IX

THE HERMIT.

WHEEL OF FORTUNE

New Chapter in Life · Change in Perspective

The wheel of fortune keeps turning - we cannot influence all events. The 4 angels of the Apocalypse and the Sphinx with the sword of fate influence the dynamics of our lives. The jackal-headed creature is reminiscent of the Egyptian god of the rites of the dead: Anubis. His primary role was overseeing the soul-balancing, and his judgment was vital. The symbols on the wheel represent the 4 elements that hold our world together.

Good times alternate with bad, time and fate are constantly rotating. It's about your own destiny, your attitude to personal fortune and the question of meaning. Ite also reminds us that there is always an opportunity, along with solutions that we cannot and do not have to influence ourselves. To do this, we should show patience and sometimes wait for the right moment until our life situation changes in our favor.

WHEEL of FORTUNE.

JUSTICE

Responsibility · Judgement · Making Decisions

The justice card leads us to confront the laws of life. It doesn't matter whether our decisions are good or bad – what matters is that we are ready to take responsibility for all conceivable consequences. Scales and sword, measuring and cutting, weighing and deciding form a unit. Every gain requires a sacrifice, every reward a small privation.

It does not help us to blame others – those who blame others give others power. Whoever bears the blame and responsibility, who is able to endure the consequences, also increases his own power and success. When making decisions, it is important to weigh these aspects. Anyone who tries to work with unfair means will fail. Justice means taking responsibility. This also includes independently checking externally imposed values and norms and being ready to question them in favor of our own sense of justice and, if necessary, to discard them.

XI

JUSTICE.

THE HANGED MAN

Trial · Resistance · New Point of View

The hanged man wants to live, but sees himself tied up and powerless. This state will continue until he realizes how useless his resistance is. As a solution, the card suggests to surrender to the situation. An uncomfortable change is necessary - often involuntarily. A completely different attitude than the previous one is required. But the sun of enlightenment signals a positive change. You will be warned of an impending sacrifice, but after you have made it, everything will turn out for the better. Watching a situation develop with no intervention can be painful - sometimes this path of conscious passivity is the wisest path. In every crisis there is also an opportunity.

The hanged man is not always able to cope with involuntary paralysis - the impatience and the desire to get out of the uncomfortable situation by force is often very strong. Internalizing the deep message of the tarot card of the hanged man requires a lot of maturity and a strong personality.

XII

THE HANGED MAN.

DEATH

Dissolving · Farewell · Closure · New Beginnings

Death stands for a painful farewell. In the end, nothing is the same as it was before. Sometimes the death tarot card also reminds us to shed part of ourselves - our old beliefs or imposed values - and just let go. Death in its entirety does not symbolize the premature end of a matter but the normal process of dying or parting.

In the context of the cards the cause of the end of a situation can usually be found, including the necessary personal discussion. The tarot card encourages the necessary process to accept the pain and the finality, as this can also result in positive aspects that set in after the change.

DEATH.

TEMPERANCE

Balance · Consistency · Facing Transience

Body, mind and soul have to be re-mixed and weighed again and again in our everyday life. The guardian angel symbolizes our spiritual power, which leads our selves into the light. We always have to weigh up how much we are willing to give or take. It all depends on the right mix – every day is different. A path leads to the sun in which the crown is located. This is the goal. We can only achieve it with the right balance of our mental components. The mixing process does not take place with a measuring cup or a strict recipe, but with a sense of proportion and intuition. The emotional balance requires a lot of flexibility from us. We always have to find a mixture with which we feel comfortable – otherwise we will poison our soul. To do this, we have to experiment anew every day and always adapt to new situations. Those who understand this message of moderation will be crowned with success at the end of their journey.

XIV

TEMPERANCE.

THE DEVIL

Egotism · Addiction · Seduction · Magic

He is a master of seduction. No one can completely escape the charm of evil. But sometimes it is necessary to break the chains imposed and to cross new boundaries. Often the card also symbolizes the weaker self, hidden enmity and chaos. But we can free ourselves from these shackles. The card inevitably reminds of the fall of man, the expulsion from paradise. Humanity as a victim of its own desires. It reminds us that not only the pursuit of purity defines our human life, but also the seduction of darkness.

We also have to face our own shadow side and sometimes submit to purer values and morals. Otherwise we will wither into chained diabolical and willless tools of our own dark side. The devil does not embody the typically bad and unholy here. Often it is precisely that which is supposedly sacred with very devilish and life-negating properties. The devil often takes on the shape of an angel of light in order to be able to seduce his victims even better.

THE DEVIL.

THE TOWER

Breakthrough · Liberation · Purification

The tower symbolizes limiting principles of our faith. The walls grow high to form an imposing royal tower. As with the tower of Babel, dogmatic opinions and views solidify. The tower no longer has a door to exit through. At some point, the lightning bolt of objective truth hits the piled up prison and brings it to collapse. A world collapses when the illusion collapses. But the divine sparks accompany the falling people as they fall into freedom. The tower reminds us that the numerous fairy tales and dogmas that affect us every day will collapse unexpectedly at some point.

Only when we are suddenly thrown out of the window of the supposed illusion do we become aware of the scope.

THE TOWER.

THE STAR

Clarity · Transparency · Truth · Beauty · Source

The star inspires creativity and the urge to create. We draw from the source of life. We feel strengthened, pulsating with heart energy, and it appears to us as if we are bathing in a refreshing spring in our soul world. The star shows us the fountain of youth. The tarot card brings luck and encourages optimism and hope. The star promises healing and success, or a positive turn.

In particular, this means a new process of consciousness. The seeds sown in the past have germinated and it's time to harvest – it's been worth the effort. The card shows us that it is time to enjoy the fruits of our labor and let our emotions run free.

XVII

THE STAR.

THE MOON

Longing · Depth · Dreams · The State of the Soul

Dog (the tamed part of us) and wolf (the wild part of us) howl longingly at the moon. We experience a longing for fulfillment, we are absorbed into our dreams and longings. Only the moon illuminates the shadowy night, only indistinct contours of things are recognizable.

The tarot card asks us to give in to our inner feelings and to give in to our longing. There is another truth behind the familiar reality. Our subconscious has already recognized it, it just hasn't risen up to our consciousness. Perhaps you have to go through a mental crisis to become conscious, at least there is still some ambiguity in one matter. The moon asks us to drop our fears and allow our deep longings to light the way in the dark.

THE MOON.

THE SUN

Energy · Happiness · Optimism · Fullfillment · Warmth

The sun provides clarity, drives away the yearnings of the night and brings us back to reality. It donates warmth and energy, a symbol of happiness, joy and success. The child sits carefree, playing on the horse, and enjoys the warmth, enjoys the flowers and feels the soothing rays of the sun on the skin. The carefreeness comes to an end again at some point when the night takes over again. But at the moment there is happiness, light and clarity. The dark is defeated and joy returns.

The sun challenges us to give our light to others, to forgive and to reconcile so that the light of the sun can move into our hearts – as an inner light for darker days.

THE SUN.

JUDGEMENT

Redemption · Renewal · Leaving the Past Behind

Follow your inner call. Follow your hunch and surrender. Judgement is not about punishment but about awakening (unborn) life. Many possibilities and abilities are hidden within us and are waiting to be awakened. The angel of judgement calls for renewal with his golden trumpet. This is about alignment with the universal principle of life. Often we also have to give up our old life and our prejudices or let them die in order to be able to renew ourselves. Every end already bears the germ of a new beginning.

The map calls us to awaken our hidden aspects of our soul and free ourselves from death. Perhaps an inner voice within us calls for a decisive change, but we have not yet had the courage to answer the call of the voice.

The judgement frees us from a death-like situation and our intuition tells us what it is primarily about, how the call is meant.

JUDGEMENT.

THE WORLD

Completion · Wholeness · Inner Peace

The world dancer unites the 4 ends of the earth, connects the opposites of the cosmos and creates universal balance. The two white sticks in her hand symbolize the united poles, the unity of the whole.

The world challenges us to use our freedom wisely. Sometimes the attainment of freedom requires breaking the boundaries, breaking through external constraints. In this way we regain our emotional balance and can in turn give this harmony to our environment. The world stands for the achievement of a goal, the final realization of our dreams and desires – the final consummation. If we have not yet reached our goal, this card signals that we are on the right track and that the reward is not far away.

XXI

THE WORLD.

MINOR ARCANA

The **four suits** of the **MINOR ARCANA** consist of the **number cards** and the **court cards** with **wands, cups, swords and pentacles.** Each of these four signs stands for an element and addresses different areas of life and levels of meaning.

Overall, the cards of the MINOR ARCANA in the tarot interpretation show everyday concerns, questions and problems. They do not show dramatic turns, but rather tendencies in our lives. Some even leave them out completely in their interpretations, but they can also provide us with important information.

ACE OF WANDS

Initiative · Opportunity · Birth · Creativity

The ace of wands stands for procreation and potential. The card symbolizes the power of inspiration from which new deeds result. The ace of wands therefore also stands for luck and a new beginning. Occasionally it warns us not to let an opportunity slip by but to seize it quickly.

It also reminds us to forge our happiness anew every day. We can have joy and fun with our goals, our personal development and the paving of a successful and happy life. To do this, however, we first have to learn to always see life a little more positively than it appears at first glance. Cape Diem – use the day, as well as your life force. The card demands activity and affirmation of life from us. We have to seize our talents and our luck and actively deal with them – otherwise we miss the chance to raise our personality and our well-being to the necessary level.

ACE of WANDS.

TWO OF WANDS

Contradiction · Addition · Two Options

Two of Wands shows us two levels of reality, the world in the background and the model of the world in the hand of the observer. The tarot card shows a low wall that allows for a vision of new challenges. The observer is still in the planning phase. Does he want to reach another continent? Does he think about the big picture in order to develop new plans from it?

The card encourages the questioner to plan carefully. He stands between the bars, between the tools, but he is still in the weighing phase. At some point he will carry out his plan, but the course has not yet been set.

Big ventures always require a healthy amount of planning and care. It also reminds us of the big difference between theory and practice – because in practice you learn of the obstacles and the details which were still unknown to us in the planning phase. The left hand on the wand – the side of the heart – tells us that this is also about the inclusion of our intuition.

II

THREE OF WANDS

Development · Walking New Paths · Accomplishing Goals

Someone has reached a hill and has a good overview of the landscape. His 3 sticks rest upright next to him while he looks at the landscape and lets the golden river with the little messengers go by. The strength is to be found in serenity. Card three of the wands encourages us to wait and not make hasty decisions. Perhaps there will be a new perspective on the company that will prove important for the future. Now is the time to watch and wait for the right time to act. The golden sky and the golden river promise a rich reward that patience will bring.

One reaches one's goal through knowledge and wisdom. Action has to be taken – that is important – but success now lies in a holistic view and preparation. Only then action is taken and success is certain. The card can also be an indication that the work and patience of the past is now paying off.

III

FOUR OF WANDS

Openness · Generosity · Bringing Clarity

The four wands are decorated and form a new gate of life. This tarot card is about breaking new ground and leaving the old one behind. Like decorated maypoles, this festive scene is reminiscent of spring, fertility and growth. The golden yellow sky promises wealth and reward.

Four of Wands is an invitation to go out – to try new things and to step through the blessed gate. The celebrants in the background greet with lively green tufts, inviting the viewer to finally take the decisive step through the festival gate. The city in the background is safe and hospitable. If you turn the invitation down you will certainly miss something, but you will not be coerced either – nobody can be forced to be happy. In summary, the viewer should gain insight: Experience the sunny side of life? Why not? Now is the time.

IV

FIVE OF WANDS

Competition · Challenge · Test of Strength

Five young men playfully fight with the 5 wands of fire. There is no blood flowing, no one is inferior – it is a mutual training to improve the strength of each individual. Everyone wears a different robe, is an individual, but the game has clearly agreed rules. You motivate each other to perform at your best, and each individual's weaknesses and strengths are put to the test in a playful way.

The card is an invitation to practice the willingness to work on our skills in a team with others. If we surround ourselves with weak and impotent people, we are also easily tempted to be weak and impotent as well. If, on the other hand, we surround ourselves with strong and motivated personalities who love the challenge, we will also mature into a strong and motivated personality.

The Five of Wands tarot card advises us not to avoid competing with others. A strong team around us – that challenges us – can playfully shorten our path to our personal goals.

V

SIX OF WANDS

Victory · Recognition · Balancing Strengths and Weaknesses

A rider with the winner's laurel wreath trots through the crowd. The rider and his horse wear the colors of life. The winner may have successfully completed a tournament or ended a competition with a win. The other 6 wands congratulate the winner's wand – the crowd stands behind the rider and his mission. Now is the time to enjoy the past toil and be rewarded. It also let in exaggerated recognition.

All in all, the card promises a positive turn of events, the victorious conclusion to an important matter.

VI

SEVEN OF WANDS

Assertiveness · Bravery · Overcoming Envy and Moral Requirements

In front of an abyss, the person fights with 6 rising fire sticks. With his staff he resolutely protects himself against the threatening wands. Seven of Wands is about warding off obstructive impulses and weaknesses. If we want to improve our situation, we also have to be ready to leave our comfort zone. The effort pays off, but before that life and we ourselves still have some resistance in store. We can only fight this fight alone.

The message of the tarot card is about the active confrontation with forces that are working against us. The solution is the conscious battle against them. The menacing wands emerge from the abyss, they appear suddenly. But the person is prepared for the situation and already has a defense staff. Thus, this tarot card also warns us to prepare for upcoming conflicts - which we may not even know of - and to be well prepared for the fight.

VII

EIGHT OF WANDS

Acceleration · News · Harmony with Nature · Limbo

Eight wands are in free fall and the landing is imminent. These sticks will hit fertile ground, take root there, and grow. Eight of Wands is a positive card. It indicates that in the immediate future something good is about to come into our lives – it will happen out of the blue and in a surprising way.

However, we need to give the wands space in our lives and be open to the events ahead. They must be allowed to fall on fertile ground with us. The sky is blue and the landscape is lively and green. With open expectations and optimism we can happily approach a positive situation. Maybe a new love, new business fields or positive news.

VIII

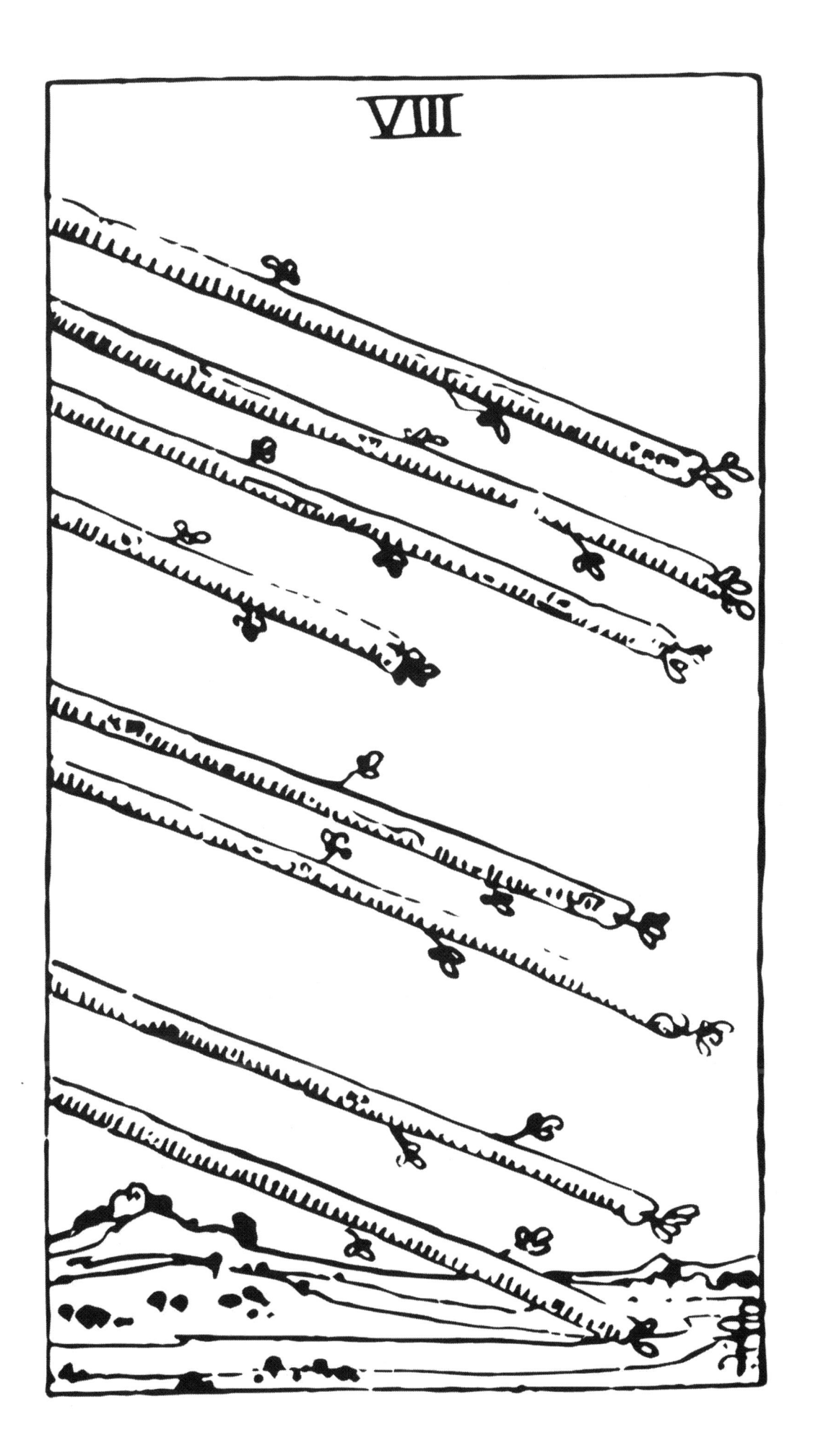

NINE OF WANDS

Overcoming Fears · Possibilities · Fullfilling One's Wishes

The person on this tarot card is wearing a head bandage, which indicates an old emotional wound. This can be an unhappy love or an insult. He's clinging to his staff and has put up a protective fence made of sticks. He isolates himself from his environment and builds a prison for himself. The wound is healed, it is time to take the bandage off again and bravely step out into the world again. It's the fear of further injury.

If they are unhappy in love, the person may be afraid of further disappointment and therefore not ready to embark on a new relationship. In your job you may have faced an unhappy work environment and therefore shy away from taking on new risks or challenges.

With its very clear imagery, Nine of Wands conveys a situation that we all know - the exaggerated fear of the new due to negative experiences in the past. Against these fears it is necessary to act with renewed courage.

IX

TEN OF WANDS

Responsibility · Purpose · A Higher Plane

The Ten of Wands tarot card can be interpreted in several ways. On the one hand, the journeyman concentrates his strength and prepares for the use of his staff. On the other hand, he seems strained and his gaze is blocked by the bars. In any case, he has big plans and moves towards houses, fields and trees.

This card suggests not to unnecessarily dissipate your strength when dealing with large goals and to concentrate on the essentials. The person has clasped the maximum number of sticks tightly and therefore only has to walk his way once. For maximum success, we need to focus on our talents and strengths, not our weaknesses. If we always want to be too perfectionist and only work on our weaknesses and mistakes, we lose sight of what is important. We can then no longer use our existing strengths effectively. In order to achieve our goals – that is the core message of this card – we have to concentrate our energies and resources on one task.

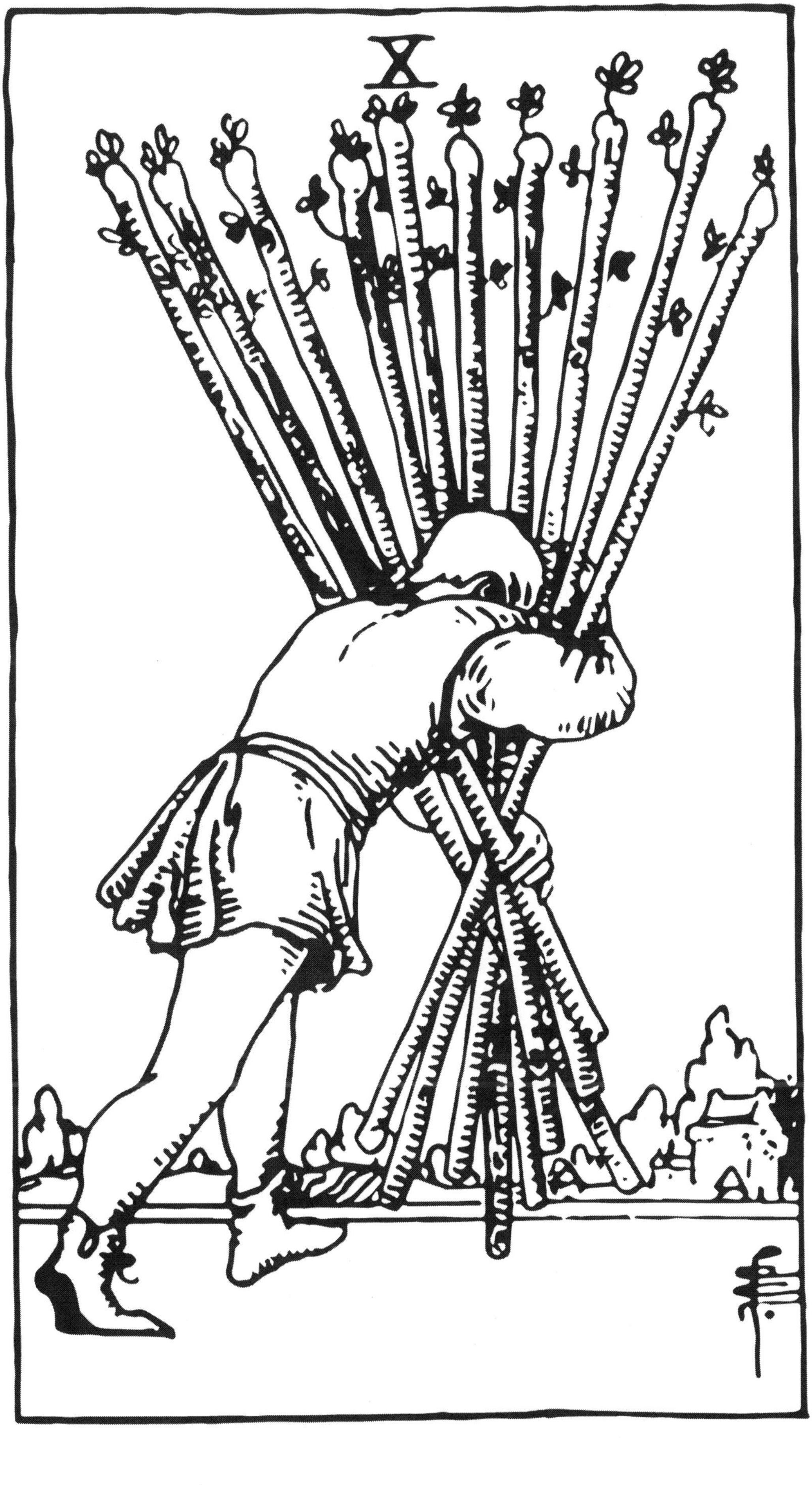
X

PAGE OF WANDS

Promise · Need for Adventure · Departure

A young man in a fire-colored robe walks through the desert. He looks at his staff with curiosity. He is free - almost like a fool - to do what he wants. He is an explorer and has the freedom to explore the world. His goal is still completely open, at some point he will cross the hills and find out where his adventure is leading him. He is always on the right track.

Sometimes we have to take the freedom to acquire completely new knowledge, to get to know new people and sometimes to shift the center of our lives. If we just focus on our safe homes, we are missing out on the opportunity to discover new talents, develop new skills, and seize significant opportunities within us.

Page of Wands is an invitation to more curiosity, flexibility and openness towards the unknown. In certain phases of life it sometimes makes more sense to keep your goals open, as the page of wands does.

PAGE of WANDS.

KNIGHT OF WANDS

Energy · Commitment · Immediate Action

Determined and full of energy, the knight of wands rides towards his goal – no obstacles hold him back. This tarot card is an invitation to a determined and joyful leap into life without fear of obstacles.

The hills in the background have the shape of pyramids, which is reminiscent of the crusaders of the Orient – with ambition, zest for action and without fear, he rides towards his goal or his project. A tarot card that calls for immediate action with the full use of all forces. Doubts about the mission are not appropriate now.

KNIGHT of WANDS.

QUEEN OF WANDS

Trust · Security · Warmth · Openness · Virtue

The card Queen of Wands combines both the male fire element and the female earth element, represented by the sunflower in her hand. This creates a balance between the gender polarities. A black cat at her feet represents feminine intuition paired with magical power. She looks down upon her realm in an upright way. Left and right two lions form the pedestals of their throne – symbols of her power. She rules stately and self-confidently with a firm grip and control. She rules with wisdom and pride, serenity and dignity.

The tarot card Queen of Wands is an invitation to approach the task at hand with self-confidence and courage. We should face the new situation fearlessly and with responsibility.

QUEEN of WANDS.

KING OF WANDS

Willpower · Aspiration · Authority · Leadership

The king of wands sits on his throne adorned with lions and salamanders and looks forward piercingly. He could rise from his throne, but his power lies in his discipline and patience. His protection animal is the fire salamander who looks in the same direction at his feet. The green color around his shoulders represents growth and vitality.

The king of wands encourages us to be patient and thereby show our power. Hasty action endangers the power of the king, who is sovereign and powerful from his rulership over his kingdom. Personal maturity and growth make us powerful and enable us to responsibly achieve our goals.

KING of WANDS

ACE OF CUPS

Celebration · Growth · Fertility

The Ace of Cups card lets the source of truth, wisdom and life flow. The original spring connects above with below, donates healing and life energy, a source of spirituality. A source of immortal being and creative power. This magical source abolishes the polarities and allows them to merge into a unity. This tarot card is a call to allow this energy to flow through you. The golden chalice with the W for wisdom and truth symbolizes the spiritual source of life full of real wealth and inspiration.

The water of life and love flows without our active involvement - we only have to be ready to drink from it. The dove stands for love, spiritual inspiration and magical energy - this tarot card also stands for the hermetic law of vibrations and magic: As above - so below, as below - so above. As inside - so outside, as outside - so inside. As in the big, so in the small. In this sense, the source also relates to our personal willpower, our feelings and the flow of our inner and outer perception.

ACE of CUPS.

TWO OF CUPS

Attraction · An Important Encounter · Clearing Up Feelings

A couple stands across from each other and toasts with the cups. The winged fiery lion hovers above them with two connected snakes – a symbol of the erotic attraction between the two.

The tarot card Two of Cups is a positive relationship card that puts an upcoming bond under a good star. The relationship is fruitful, fair and will stand on a solid foundation over a long period of time. Both sign a contract by clinking their cups, both accept the rights and obligations that result from the mutual connection. This step will be the first step for both of them into a happy, passionate and fruitful relationship.

In general, Two of Cups can also symbolize a business contract, a new goal, or a compromise between two possibilities. In all of these cases – where a connection is created between two polarities – it boils down to a positive end result that is of great benefit to both sides – a classic win-win situation.

II

THREE OF CUPS

Gratitude · Joy · Fullfillment · Recovery

At this celebration, three women toast each other. All around them are rich fruits, the sky is blue and free of clouds - they dance happily. They form a circle to describe the great cycle of life, nature and the cosmos.

Life is a dynamic river with high and deep waves, with good times and bad. The Three of Cups tarot card is about the good times when the labors of labor and sowing are rewarded with a bountiful harvest. The three women are certainly an allusion to mother nature and the earth goddess Gaia, who, together with the warming sun, is the basis of all life. It is now time to celebrate, enjoy the results of the sacrifices made, and share that joy with others as well.

Three of the cups convey the message that the work that has been done is now paying off joyfully.

III

FOUR OF CUPS

Reorientation · Coming Back to Yourself · Finding Your Way Out of a Crisis

A man sits lost in thought under a tree and looks into space. He closes himself off from his environment, remains passive and introverted. His arms and legs are crossed – he rejects any action and proactivity. He does not pay attention to the three cups in front of him, he even ignores the fourth cup, which is offered to him directly from heaven – he would only have to grab it to drink from the fullness of life.

We often feel like this person in Four of Cups. We're too busy with ourselves and miss out on valuable offers. This can be a valuable opportunity to meet good people in our environment or to start a new path.

In order to fully exploit our potential, we cannot remain inactive forever – life invites us to use our talents and to face new challenges. The card Four of Cups challenges us to finally fully develop our dormant potential.

IV

FIVE OF CUPS

Pain · Grief · Disappointments · New Beginnings

A turned away person in the black robe of mourning. Quiet, straight and lost in thought, they look nowhere. It is still time to process sad feelings, digest setbacks and deal with the emptiness that has arisen. During this time we do not register the rich river right in front of our feet, the bridge and the world behind it. Unfortunately, we then only see three buried goblets, the wealth of which we perceive as irretrievable loss. We stand behind a "line of retreat" that we have produced.

Mental wounds just need their time to heal - we should take this time calmly. When the time of grief is over, we will raise our heads again and open ourselves to the abundance around us. We then turn around and see the remaining goblets that are still full, which are just waiting to be used by us. We will recognize the world and its possibilities again and take the first step towards the bridge.

V

SIX OF CUPS

Pleasure · Joy · Memory · Nostalgia

A scene that seems unreal at first glance. A boy gives a little girl a present – a representation as though in a fairy tale. Is it a declaration of love, a thank you or just an unexpected gift. The chalice with the white flowers will not be the only one, the next gifts are already waiting on the pedestal in the foreground. The white flowers represent elegance and purity.

The child is an indication of old memories of our past – the coming gift has to do with our intuition in connection with the past or our childhood. Dreamy or romantic feelings have to do with it. The guard in the background leaves the two of them alone – together with the strong city walls, the picture conveys security and security.

The Six of Cups tarot card is an announcement for an aspect of the past.

VI

SEVEN OF CUPS

Surpassing Yourself · Getting the Success You Deserve

A shadowy person is blinded by imaginary goblets with jewels, gold and riches. They are castles in the air, mysterious temptations. You can see them, but they remain imaginary. They are fantastic dreams that arise out of wishful thinking.

The Seven of Cups tarot card warns of the dangers of unrealistic dreams and desires. Some visions have the power of our longing on their side and they also have a strong visionary, invigorating character, but not to be underestimated are the dangers that an ambiguous wish without a sense of reality brings with it.

If we want to make our dreams come true, we must first have an idea and a picture of them – that is correct! But our wishes cannot be realized without clarification and without our deliberate action.

VII

EIGHT OF CUPS

Taking Stock · Freeing Yourself · Going Your Own Way

The hiker is on his way and painfully leaves eight goblets behind. In front of him lies a dark mountain that has yet to be overcome. He does not know what exactly to expect – there is a solar eclipse at the moment – the moon moves in front of the sun and causes darkness and obscurity.

Often unforeseen news and events slide into our lives and cloud our otherwise clear view of the goal. At the same time, Eight of Cups tells us that this state can only be temporary – at some point the moon disappears again and the light of the sun illuminates our path as usual. Sometimes we have to take risks despite uncertainty and also leave behind some security and wealth in order to be able to achieve our goal. The hiker has already overcome smaller obstacles, such as the river, and there is still a stretch to go. The tarot card Eight of Cups wants to encourage us to continue on our way despite the hardships and the current uncertainty.

VIII

NINE OF CUPS

Fullfillment · Conclusion · Relaxation

A person sits with folded arms in front of his nine piled up goblets. The cups are at head level – a sign of spiritual and emotional wealth. It gives him some power, he proudly shows his possessions to underpin his status.

The card Nine of Cups encourages us to enjoy our efforts and the goals we have achieved, and also to share our feelings with others – provided we enjoy them too. Not only emotional wealth but also joie de vivre, security and maturity are represented by this tarot card.

The person's white robe signals openness and a clear conscience. He achieved his goal through efforts and the use of experience. Certainly he will accumulate more (emotional) wealth, but he is also able to enjoy the successes on his life path. The simple wooden bench he is sitting on signals that he has been frugal in the past – maybe he will soon swap the bench for a more comfortable chair.

IX

TEN OF CUPS

Satisfaction · Energy · Joy

The tarot card Ten of Cups stands for satiety in the ideal world. A couple and two children greet the rainbow. The rich green of the landscape and the cozy country house radiate harmony. There has been a thunderstorm in the past - maybe an argument or other problems - but now the clouds have moved and a colorful rainbow appears with 10 rich goblets.

The tarot card Ten of Cups sends us the message that the turbulent times are now over - everything is alright again now. Ten is a divine number that expresses perfection - ten fingers make two complete healthy hands. This includes interpersonal relationships, the financial situation and our well-being.

No negative or disruptive influences can be seen on the entire map - including no hidden warnings. If we are currently still seeing clouds overhead and standing in the rain, Ten of Cups promises us that our subconscious already suspects better times.

X

PAGE OF CUPS

Helpfulness · A Friendly Gesture · Important Event

The boy stands in front of a sea of feelings and impressions. A cup is in his hand and a fish looks at him. The fish comes from an area of life that seems closed off to us humans – many of its secrets and inhabitants are still completely unexplored. The fish is associated with mysticism, fertility and wealth. He is trapped in the golden cup, waiting for the boy's decision.

The Page of Cups tarot card invites us to face a completely new situation with curiosity. Unbelief is punished, faith is rewarded. It is about the ocean of our soul, the deep feelings and beliefs that are still hidden in our subconscious. It is important to fathom these and gratefully accept the new possibilities.

The Page of Cups is a predominantly positive card that encourages us to see the interesting new situation as useful – to willingly face the new feelings without prejudice and fears.

PAGE of CUPS.

KNIGHT OF CUPS

Inspiration · Idealism · Harmony Between Knowledge and Feelings

Like the other court cards of cups, the knight is related to the flowing water. Fish decorate his armor – he is a knight in search of the holy grail, the primordial ground of being. He explores the flow of his soul, truth and spirituality. He rides towards truth and wisdom, his gaze fixed on his goal – his golden goblet points in the direction of his path, which he rides purposefully with his white horse.

The card Knight of Cups is an invitation to seek, explore, strive for and perfect our purpose in life, our identity and our emotional diversity again and again. The tarot card is a sign that our goal consists of numerous sub-steps.

Only those who are ready to dive into the abyss of their own self will also be able to successfully face new challenges in the materialistic world. The path you have chosen leads in the right direction, there are no obstacles on the way, but the card also prompts you not to stop.

KNIGHT of CUPS.

QUEEN OF CUPS

Honesty · Wisdom · Gentleness

The queen of cups looks at her magnificent goblet of wisdom with fascination, interest and inspiration. Her sea blue robe merges with the sea in front of her shell throne. She knows the changing currents, the ebb and flow of life and her soul. It forms the connection between the realm of the earth and the water. But the cup is much more – it is a holy ark with a high, spiritual secret inside – this is symbolized by the two inconspicuous cherubs on both sides of the chalice.

The queen of cups rules both the energies of the soul and the material realm. In every second of our life we have to align our soul life with everyday experiences. Letting the devotion and the waves of emotion flow is the key this tarot card aims to teach us. The point here is to focus on our sensitivity, personal spirituality and intuition. Our mental health and its balance are never subordinate to the material world. It is important to protect them and to worship them with devotion.

QUEEN of CUPS.

KING OF CUPS

Passion · Tenderness · Maturity · Sentimentality

The king of cups sits in the water of his emotions. The throne creates the necessary distance between him and the water, connects the element of air with the realm of the soul. He is the master of his feelings, placing himself in the center without subordinating himself to the water.

Feelings are not controlled by our consciousness but arise from the source of the subconscious. We gain the necessary authority over the unfathomable realm of our emotions through self-confidence, effort and the conscious confrontation with them. We have to transmute the incomprehensible and intangible waters of emotions into something controllable.

The King of Cups is a direct invitation to become the ruler of our emotions by connecting with them at the same time and yet creating the necessary distance. This includes constantly working on our self-reflection and putting our decisions and feelings on a solid foundation.

KING of CUPS.

ACE OF SWORDS

Clarity · Triumph · Exaggeration

A lofty sword takes control of the space of the air. The cards of swords are subordinate to the element air – the element of clarity, thinking and conscious perception. The sword in the tarot symbolizes keen intellect, assertiveness, strong will and unstoppable fate. A sword is the most important offensive weapon in close combat.

The Ace of Swords is about the sharp mind crowned with sovereignty. This is about independent thoughts, free creativity and the release of one's own spiritual potential and power. This potential is supported by spirituality and willpower.

The Ace of Swords in tarot gives us courage to exhaust our spiritual potential and promises decisive new ideas. Thoughts are free and those who use their keen intellect can better protect themselves from untruths and manipulation in the flood of information.

ACE of SWORDS.

TWO OF SWORDS

Conversations · Discussions · Becoming Conscious of the Unconscious

A man in a white robe with blindfolded eyes and two swords in the moonlight. This representation on the waters of the soul under cover of darkness is the epitome of concentration. The two swords offer protection and express a warning - don't bother me, I want to be alone with my thoughts. Those who close their eyes look into their own depths of the soul. It is about gaining knowledge from the inner self.

The tarot card Two of Swords conveys the message to concentrate on your own inspirations, feelings and beliefs. Doubts and insecurities arise from within and can only be fought there. This at the same time passive and active attitude enables the expansion of one's own intuition, which is not yet accessible in this scene. A pure attitude that only interprets influences and impressions from the outside world does not lead any further at the moment, as the harmonious balance between the inside and the outside has not yet been established.

II

THREE OF SWORDS

Understanding · Reason · Seperation · Lovesickness

A single heart and many tears – the difficulty runs deep and cannot be ignored. It is an emotional pain because there is no blood flowing. Dealing with this pain is also healing.

The Three of Swords tarot card indicates the need for spiritual healing. This process takes time and a conscious approach to the situation. The swords must first be pulled out of the heart so that permanent healing is possible – the pain must therefore be processed consciously. Sure, others can alleviate the pain by listening, but the heart is still quite lonely. Coping with the situation requires the greatest effort on the part of the sufferer himself.

In addition to lovesickness, this card is also about acting against the emotional will. This can either be a necessary rational step or it can mean the opposite: do not trust your own intuition. The context of the cards is important for this.

III

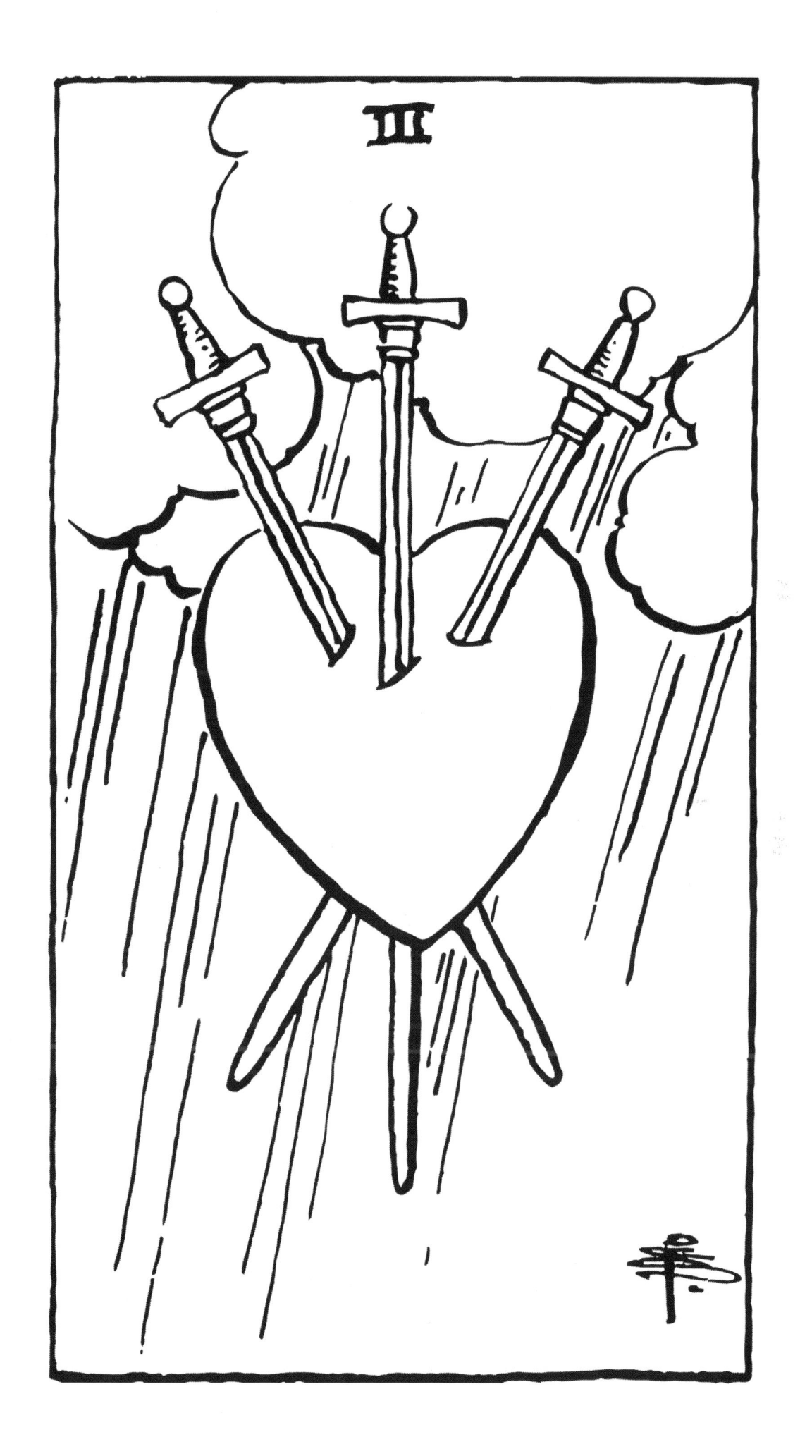

FOUR OF SWORDS

Standstill · Taking a Break · Reflection

Like a cast statue, a person apparently lies asleep on a pedestal or grave. But he does not sleep – his hands are pointed to the sky like a sword, forming a triangle. Three swords hang over him and point to his upper body – he lets razor-sharp insights and thoughts affect him. In the immersion and in the calm he releases himself from the captivity of the first person perspective. He lets his mind leave the material body for a short time in order to gain an expanded view from the meta-level. Out of retreat and calm he gains strength, remains waiting, observing and reflecting. Now is the time to step back and be open to inspiration. Intuition and clarity are required now, the struggle and the material tasks are only in the future, until the right moment has come.

The tarot card Four of Swords shows the importance of inner concentration in order to gain new knowledge – before the knowledge gained can be put into practice.

IV

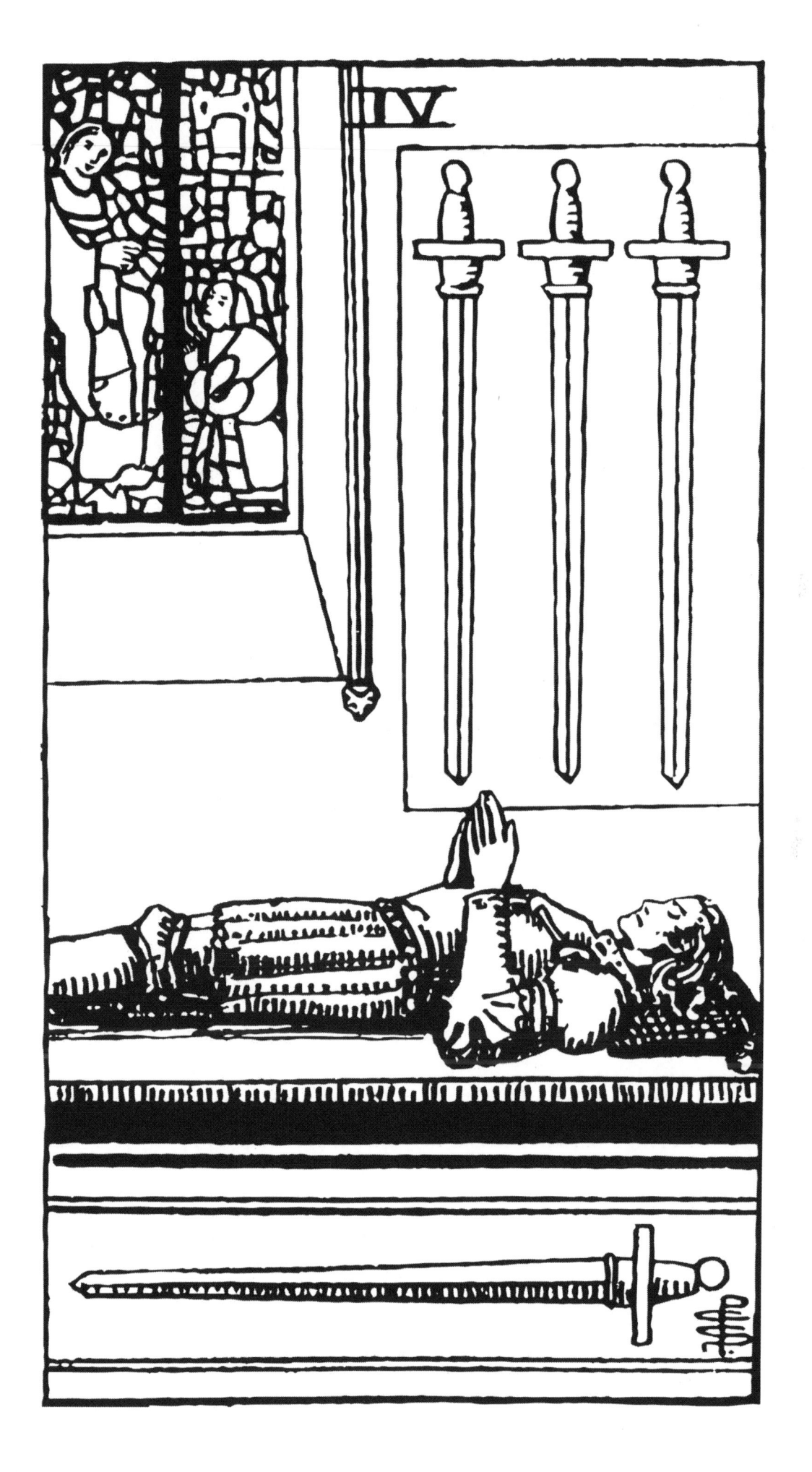

FIVE OF SWORDS

Defeat · Failure · Change · Learning From the Past

Pieces of clouds chase across the sky, the sea is in motion. The person has three swords with him, one figure leaves the place, another stands depressed directly at the water. Two swords lie on the ground at his feet. What happened? A quarrel or a fight with disarmament? Or was the depicted person attacked by robbers and was able to disarm and force them to surrender? Another possibility is that the conflict started with the person in the foreground.

The tarot card Five of Swords admonishes us to sleep one more night before a direct conflict and to consider carefully whether we will dare another fight or be satisfied with the partial victory. In any case, the card is an indication that we must reckon with a confrontation in which one will not be squeamish with one another. It also calls on us to examine whether the use of the funds is worth the result.

V

SIX OF SWORDS

Breaking Free From Constraints · Reorientation · Departure

Two people, whose faces we do not recognize, cross a large body of water with six swords. You leave a lot behind, but you are prepared for any further conflict. The other bank is already in sight. The Six of Swords tarot card prepares us for a change. We have to leave our previous soul world and comfort zone, give up our old home and face a completely new situation. It is a new beginning, but we are not alone – there are one or more people who will accompany us on our new journey and share our fate with us. The sky is clear – we will eventually find our way into the new situation.

But it is a painful farewell – from an old hope, a goal that is important to us or from old outdated values. Perhaps our previous view of the world has collapsed and our journey into the new situation has not yet been completed. We are also faced with the truth of a new situation here. First we have to make sacrifices and let go of much of what we have seen as our home. Soon we will reach the new shore, realize new plans and goals.

VI

SEVEN OF SWORDS

Walking Your Own Path · Liberation · Unconventional ideas

A person with five swords sneaks away from a camp. He had to leave two swords behind – these form a boundary between himself and the camp. Is he a thief who robbed an enemy's arsenal to weaken its defense? Or is he a soldier himself who is deserting and leaving the camp with five swords for his own defense and as loot?

Our intuition and the neighboring cards in the placement system tell us exactly what is meant. A robbery takes place and the robber wants to remain undetected. Something is stolen that weakens our defenses, but two swords remain in our possession.

The tarot card Seven of Swords prepares us for a situation in which we have to reckon with cunning or insincerity in some form, or in which we are insincere to ourselves. It is a secret and cunningly calculated situation. No matter how it turns out – we still have two swords left for defense that we can use – so there is still hope even if we were not able to recognize the dangerous situation in time.

VII.

EIGHT OF SWORDS

Dependency · External Control · Bias

The young woman stands tied and blindfolded between eight swords stuck into the ground. This card is an indication of strong blockages, a lack of intuition and powerlessness. The possibility of action is lacking and the situation can be seen through. It is not voluntary impotence – the eight swords indicate violent action. This violence can also emanate from oneself by blocking oneself and not allowing a necessary development. The rock and the old walls in the background seem stuck and rigid – an indication of stuck beliefs and a lack of foresight. The sky is gray, the ground muddy and soggy – there is a lack of firm hold and inner stability.

The tarot card Eight of Swords signals a phase of perseverance until you are ready to break free from your bonds and allow your free view again. The current rigidity and impotence will not last forever, but now it is a matter of holding out for a while and getting through the situation.

VIII

NINE OF SWORDS

Overcoming Fear · Ending Conflicts

A man wakes up from a terrible dream or is worried about not being able to sleep in the first place. The hands in front of his face block his view of the red roses on his blanket. The nine swords of fate hover over him – pointing to an unknown future. He is afraid of the fear. Darkness and horror envelop his soul.

The tarot card Nine of Swords describes the current uncertain situation of fear – and asks us to bring light and hope back into our lives – the nightmare is over. The last step left is simply to take your hands away from your eyes so that we can direct our energy forward again. We have to take this step ourselves, because the night is not over yet, the illuminating light of the sun has not yet returned. Perhaps in the current situation it is not yet clear to us that circumstances will improve again and that we must take the initiative ourselves.

IX

TEN OF SWORDS

Necessary End · Low Point · Detachment From the Past

A person pierced by ten swords – nailed down and passed out. An overly clear representation of powerlessness. Beliefs, wrong ideas and fanatical ways of thinking can put us in a state of immobility in our personality development. The person in the tarot card Ten of Swords no longer has a functioning spine, the whole body of the person is affected – the abdomen, chest, heart and head are incapable of acting. In this situation there is no longer any initiative, power or even wishful thinking – the worst possible situation a person can find themselves in. He can no longer free himself from this situation on his own. So the card can mean that we need the help of people who mean well with us, correct our beliefs and suggest alternatives – even if that (pulling out the numerous swords) in turn causes pain.

The tarot card also offers reason for hope – the darkness is already dissolving on the horizon and clears the view of a golden clear sky. If we accept the help, a golden time and healing will soon be upon us.

X

PAGE OF SWORDS

News · Plans · Spying · Observation

The page of swords whirls his sword through the air, looking for new tasks and solutions. He turns lightly and is oriented and capable of acting in all directions.

The tarot card Page of Swords is an invitation to explore new ideas, to take the initiative and to be ready at any time to tackle new tasks. The page still looks uncertain in places, concentrates for a moment on a point near him. But his view is clear and he is ready to face the new situation. His brave demeanor will prevent many opponents from even starting a fight with the page of swords.

PAGE of SWORDS.

KNIGHT OF SWORDS

Logic · Debate · Criticism · Rethinking

The knight of swords charges with his visor open and his sword raised – nothing can stop him. His armor protects the entire body, a fiery red cloak confirms his strength and power.

The knight's gaze is directed straight ahead to his target – he looks neither to the right nor to the left – nothing can distract him from the mission. The knight is fully aware of his intentions. Everyone should know what he is about to do and be careful. Whoever is not for him is against him.

KNIGHT of SWORDS.

QUEEN OF SWORDS

Independence · Loneliness · Justice · Intellect

The queen of swords holds her sword straight into the clear sky. She has just cut the red ribbon on her hand, her gaze is directed to the future, on her throne she turns her back on the past. The sky is blue and clear. Her hand points in the direction of her gaze. Her white dress confirms her openness to what comes next. She is ready to face a new future with the sword of the Spirit raised.

Sovereign and under the sign of the butterfly, the symbol of transformation into something new and better, she transforms her mind into something higher. Freed from an outdated view of things, it shows strength and power. In her new life she is the ruler of a new realm of clarity. On this tarot card she leaves doubts and paralyzing feelings behind.

QUEEN of SWORDS.

KING OF SWORDS

Intelligence · Law · Politics · Strictness

Turning his gaze to us, the king of swords expresses his firm intentions. With his sword slightly tilted towards the sky, he allows himself to be guided by spirit and wisdom. The sky is clear, the wind has subsided and the last clouds are just clearing. He sits on the throne of the butterfly, the symbol of transformation. Like a caterpillar pupates and turns into a graceful butterfly, he is currently transforming his mind. His attitude is passive, sovereign and symbolic. His clear blue robe expresses gentleness and openness, his purple cloak expresses power and assertiveness. His attitude also expresses consistency, no carelessness and also no exaggerated rushed zeal.

The tarot card King of Swords recommends to master our tasks responsibly and with care. With a keen mind and a good dose of wisdom, we rule the kingdom of our lives. We know that only we can take responsibility for our path in life. With maturity and the necessary calm, we master the current situation.

KING of SWORDS.

ACE OF PENTACLES

Satisfaction · Prosperity · Wealth

A heavenly hand gives us a precious gold coin with a pentagram on it. The pentagram symbolizes the human being and the area of our earth with the number five. It also symbolizes our five senses.

The earth is the element of the coin row. The earth gives life, growth and sensuality. The tarot card Ace of Pentacles invites us to step through the gate of abundance and to get the best out of our lives. Life is a gift to be used.

ACE of PENTACLES.

TWO OF PENTACLES

Giving Things More Attention · Looking at Possibilities From All Sides

A juggler is balancing two coins, while behind him the whipped waves of the sea are raging. The sky, on the other hand, is clear and completely cloudless. The infinity sign, the lemniscate, symbolizes that the dual forces have to be brought into harmony again and again. It is also a symbol of the law of magic that everything in the universe – the small and the large, the above and the below, male and female – form part of a single unit – everything is connected with everything and influences one another.

This tarot card is about our emotional balance. The sea of our soul is constantly exposed to the forces of the tides of the polarities. We experience high phases and low phases, negative and positive, sometimes trusting our analytical mind more and sometimes our intuition. Even if it is necessary to emphasize one pole more from situation to situation, we always have to keep both sides in balance.

II

THREE OF PENTACLES

Talent · Profession · Vocation · Business

Three people with different abilities are working to complete a pillar with three pentacles. This tarot card is an invitation to do a special task as a team. It can also be interpreted in such a way that we should resort to the competencies of other people. An abbot gives the job, an architect plans the building and the stonemason puts the task into practice – everyone has their special gifts and talents. Everyone can do something that someone else needs right now.

The three pentacles on the column are not yet gold-plated – this task is still to be done. An indication of a task that has already started and needs to be completed. This is not necessarily a physical job to be done – our personal spiritual development can also be expressed through the imagery of this tarot card. In this case we can turn to other people who have already successfully completed part of their spiritual path. The tarot card Three of the Pentacles is an invitation to rely on others for our goal, to delegate tasks and to make use of the skills of different people.

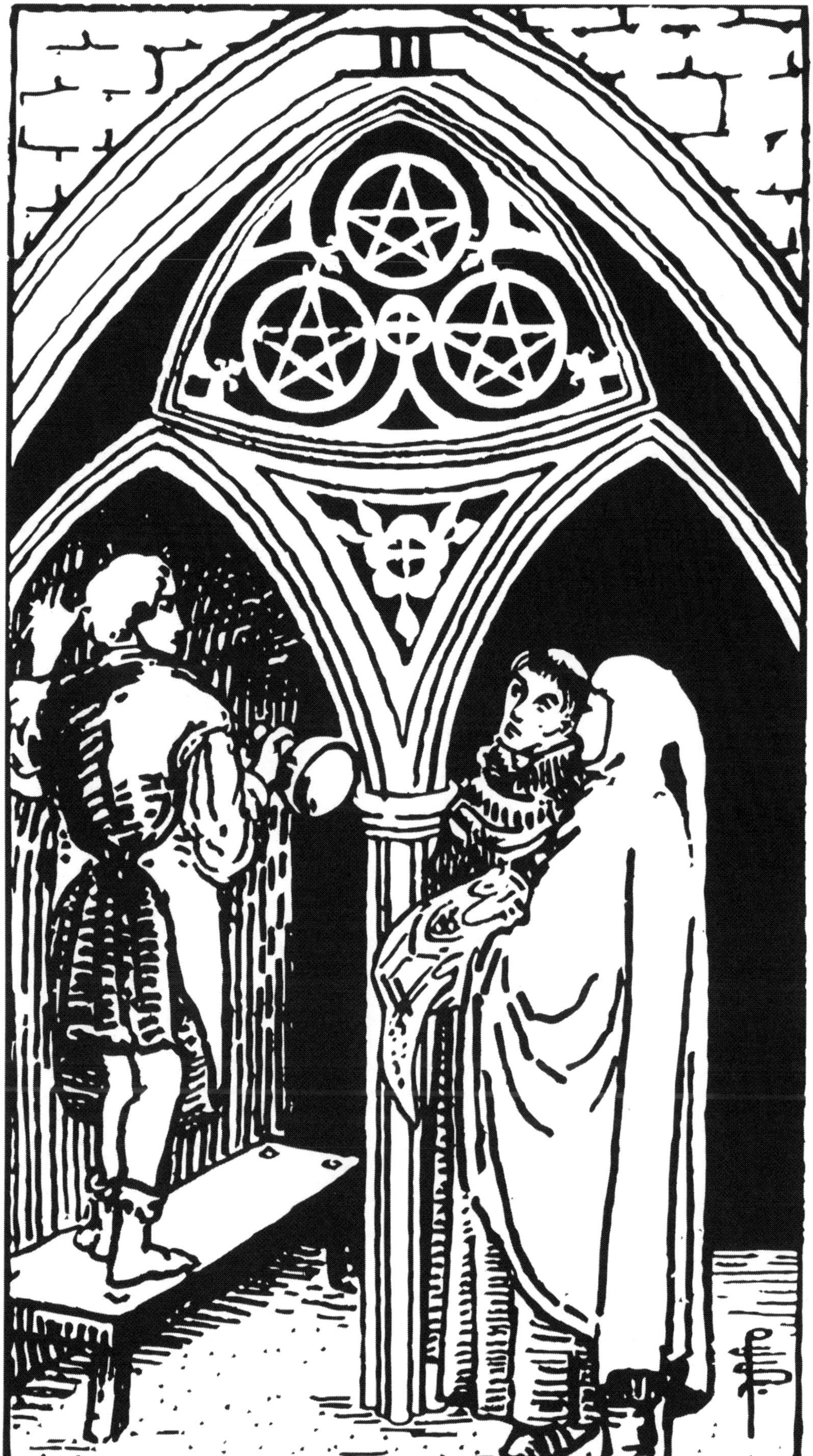

FOUR OF PENTACLES

Possession · Financial Stability · Security

A little king sits in front of his little town and guards four coins. He holds a coin in the area around his heart – an indication of inner values that need to be preserved, but at the same time this gesture also closes his heart. Another coin elevates his crown – his thoughts mainly revolve around material things. Two coins lie on the ground as a base for his feet. The little king relies on the tangible, the acquired, on clear values.

The tarot card Four of the Pentacles is an invitation to protect your intentions, actions and beliefs, but also to reconsider if necessary. The lack of sacred buildings in the city in the background also suggests an analytical and factual development. The card encourages us to continue to defend and protect our inner values in the current phase of life. At the same time, however, it also warns against concentrating too much on outward appearances and material possessions.

IV

FIVE OF PENTACLES

Poverty · Hardship · Suffering

Two figures wrapped in rags trudge through the snow. Behind them the warm glowing church window with five pentacles. It looks like a sacred building, a symbol for values and norms, social conventions. Perhaps the impoverished figures have chosen their situation voluntarily, perhaps they are simply not allowed to enter into social acceptance. This tarot card shows us a situation of isolation, a feeling of being excluded. The figures are cold and desperate to find a way back to convention to make them feel better. You are not alone, but you can only help each other to a limited extent. The two people have to keep looking for a better situation for them, they have to move on.

This card is about the negative consequences of isolation. We have to decide which path to take. The difficult situation at the moment may also have its advantages – it may be the price of freedom, independence, or the only way to escape from a golden prison. In any case, the situation is initially uncomfortable and will remain so until the snow has melted again.

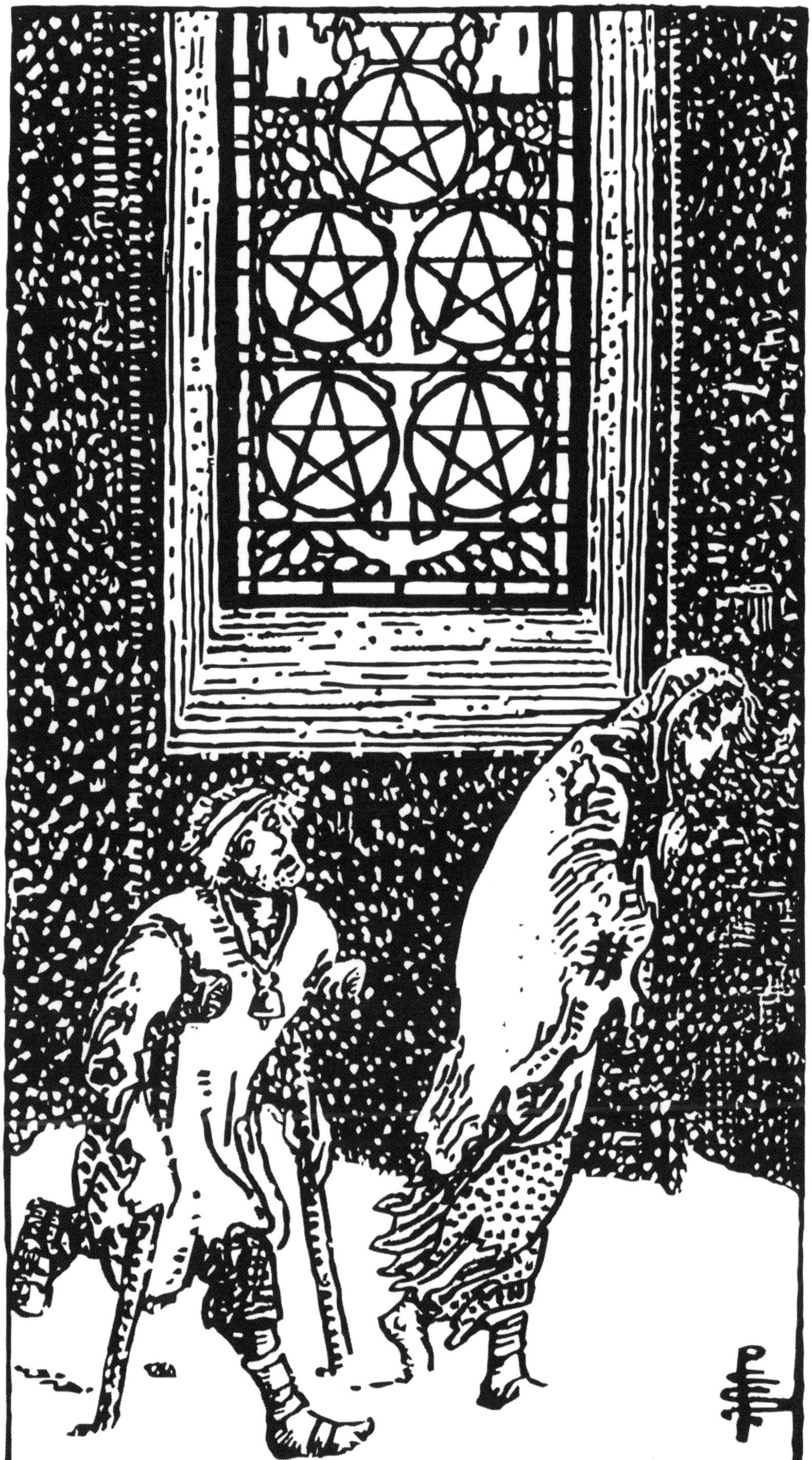

SIX OF PENTACLES

Balance · Relaxation · Luxury

A well-dressed man with a pair of scales hands a kneeling person a few coins. Another kneeling person asks for some money as well.

One is only able to give when one is ready to receive something. What is easier? To give something from a lofty position or to receive something from a humble attitude? Giving is often easier than receiving. The giver always wins something back - recognition, honor and gratitude. The recipient becomes the debtor and subordinates himself to the giver. In doing so, the giver has to weigh up exactly how he distributes his gifts.

The card Six of Pentacles reminds us of the importance of balancing taking and giving. It is also a warning that the recipient sometimes has to make the greater sacrifice, even if he is rewarded with money for it.

VI

SEVEN OF PENTACLES

Surprises or Signs From the Past

The gardener is looking at his lush bush with six of the pentacles. He leans on his tools, takes a break and enjoys the shine of the coins, the reward for his work. A small plant with a single coin fruit is right in front of him, he knows that this plant that has just been planted will also grow into a splendid shrub with many coins. But this young plant wants to be watered, cared for and kept free of weeds. If we neglect it, it will perish and not bear golden fruit. This little plant represents our present. The future has not yet been ordered - what awaits us here depends on our decisions today.

Every now and then you have to enjoy your previous successes and thus recharge your batteries for new things - that is one of the central statements of the tarot card Seven of Pentacles. We are asked to realize what our strengths are. If we only focus on our weaknesses we just get stuck. At the moment we have to focus on our strengths and what we have achieved so far - this is the only way to gain courage and enthusiasm for new, fruitful projects.

VII

EIGHT OF PENTACLES

Fruitful Work · Success

The craftsman works the eighth pentacle with devotion. Five hang raised on a tree, another is still leaning against a stool, another is lying next to him in the dust for refinement. His attention belongs to the one he is currently working on.

The tarot card Eight of Pentacles wants to motivate us to complete the work we have started – our goal, our development or the realization of an idea. Others can already marvel at our talent. With every blow of the hammer we come a little closer to the completion of the workpiece. But we not only work on the workpiece but also on ourselves at the same time. Our unique talents want to be challenged, expanded and used for our own benefit and that of others. Even if our work is often tedious and monotonous – with every movement we become a little richer. The energies want to flow through us, want to encourage us to grow beyond ourselves.

The card is an invitation for continuous self-improvement – the effort will be worth it.

VIII

NINE OF PENTACLES

Hidden Talents · Results of Creation

A person of high standing walks gracefully through their lush garden. It bears abundant fruits. The person unites the opposites – the fast hawk on their hand and the slow snail in the garden at their feet. The person's robe is also golden yellow and decorated with venus-like flowers. Her inner world connects with the outer – she is ONE with her golden garden. She confidently talks to the falcon, her right hand leaning on her splendid bush of pentacles.

This tarot card is about feminine qualities – the combination of soulful intuition, patience and creativity. Card Nine of Pentacles also shows us that a situation needs both skill and a sense of the moment's grace – a very positive card that gives an indication of good decisions in the past and encourages us to continue on this path.

IX

TEN OF PENTACLES

Practical Skills · Contributions to the World · Stability · Security

The Ten of Pentacles tarot card contains several hidden messages and secrets for the initiates of esoteric symbols. A man and a woman are talking under an archway, a child is petting one of the two dogs and looks shyly at an old man, his function as a magician can be recognized by the symbols on his robe. The blue clear sky symbolizes clarity and harmony of the whole. The city walls radiate security and order. The scales and the coat of arms of the wall stand for justice and authority. The arrangement of the pentacles contains a peculiarity – the ten coins are arranged in the same structure as the Sephiroth of the Kabbalah, the Hebrew secret doctrine.

The card challenges us to take in the many small details of life within us. It's about the connection between our inner and outer values and the connection between intuition and our analytical thinking. Overall, this tarot card expresses the central need to bring the inner world and the outer world into harmony on the way to spiritual maturity.

X

PAGE OF PENTACLES

Gift · Offer

The young man holds the coin at head level with both hands. The sky is golden yellow and exudes wealth. The ground is earthy, the field is cultivated, powerful trees round off the landscape. In the background, a mountain invites the viewer to look into the distance. The boy admires the coin with dignity and strength, admires himself and symbolizes his respect for his own inner and outer wealth. The tilled field in the background and the earth-colored drapery stand for growth and maturity, but the plants still need some time and we too have to develop ourselves first, recognize and perfect our values. The blood-red headgear signals his readiness to fight for his goals.

This card is about one's own worth in connection with self-esteem. Just like the page holds up his coin, we should respect our own talents and abilities in this situation, appreciate our own worth. Only after a phase of positive self-reflection do we develop an increased sense of self-worth and are thus equipped to achieve and fulfill our goals and tasks.

PAGE of PENTACLES.

KNIGHT OF PENTACLES

Reliability · Perseverance · Hard Work · Diligence

A knight on a jet black horse holds up his coin with his visor open. In front of him lies a freshly tilled field. The sky is golden yellow and exudes mystical wealth. The mountains and the trees in the background can hardly be seen. The view of the horizon is free and clear.

The Knight of Pentacles can also be called the Knight of Loyalty and Growth. A positive matter or situation is growing. Now all that is needed is protection and patience – nature will do the rest. If the knight were impatient to ride out into the country, he would destroy part of the harvest with his hooves. The knight of pentacles shows a strong and solid character. He is true to his values, he is someone you can rely on. He is neither overly neat and tidy nor careless or lazy.

When we find ourselves in a special situation with an open outcome, this tarot card tells us that it is time to wait and see and let things take their course – there will be a ripe harvest in the end.

KNIGHT of PENTACLES.

QUEEN OF PENTACLES

Wealth · Quiet · Closeness to Nature · Healing Power · Fertility

In the midst of the lush nature, the queen of pentacles sits gracefully on her throne. The sky is golden yellow and rich, around her head are strong tendrils with red and black flowers. The mountains on the horizon flow like waves through the landscape. The queen's throne is intricately decorated and solid. Like a mother holding her baby in her arms, she carefully and caringly carries the golden coin.

The queen of pentacles symbolizes the cycle of nature, mother earth. Her robe shows the red and green of life, the white and gold of birth, the black flowers above her symbolize passing away. The cycle of life includes rebirth, life and passing away. She humbly shows her respect for these laws of the universal cycle.

This tarot card indicates a kind, down-to-earth woman or a sensual and fruitful situation. We should accept the things that come our way and fit into the great cycle of life.

QUEEN OF PENTACLES

KING OF PENTACLES

Successful Businessman · Possession · Pleasure · Envy

A rich king sits surrounded by bulls' heads with a scepter and a coin within the lush nature. He is experiencing a rich harvest. The golden yellow sky signals spiritual wealth and authority. In the background you can see a castle with many towers – a symbol of his authority and power.

The King of Pentacles tarot card represents a mature character who has worked for independence and success. His barely recognizable armor suggests that he has shown great courage and good diplomacy in the past. He is invulnerable, knows what he wants and subordinates himself to the great task.

The card explains to us that perseverance and prudent action combined with a lot of patience are often necessary to achieve our goals. Once one has reached their goal, they can enjoy the sunny side of life and let others participate in it. But this only works if they have made mostly wise decisions beforehand.

KING of PENTACLES.

Printed in Great Britain
by Amazon